MANIPULATED MEMORIES

MANIPULATED MEMORIES

S. E. ANTHONY

NEW DEGREE PRESS

COPYRIGHT © 2021 S. E. ANTHONY

All rights reserved.

MANIPULATED MEMORIES

ISBN

978-1-63730-432-7   *Paperback*
978-1-63730-521-8   *Kindle Ebook*
978-1-63730-522-5   *Digital Ebook*

to my mom,
for hiding poetry where I'd find it

to my ancestors,
for nothing grows without the roots

to my sister,
for being everything right with the world

to those who inspired it
and will never read it

and to the one
who taught me unconditional love
(you know who you are)

CONTENTS

my grandma once told me she was still alive
because people still think of her.
to me,
that meant every breath she took reflected someone
in the world having her in mind and spirit.
thoughts immortalized her.
that's the legacy i want to leave and the life i want to live.
for every breath i take, i want someone to be walking
in a word i spoke, laugh i left, and love i openly gave.
i crafted this book to do just that.
to leave a piece of me with my readers forever.

—

in this collection, i peel back the layers of the growth
that is possible after destruction. i explore the deranged
reality of battling with oneself, and i talk myself out
of death and heartbreak time and time again.
this book is an open love letter to everyone.
whether it's lost love, battling mental health, or
seeking answers in lonely places, this is for you.
i want you to see this book as an opportunity
to explore your inner self, your healing,
and your memories in a new light.
i applaud you for finally
seeking out voices that speak to who you are becoming
—stepping into your power.
the best thing you can do for yourself
is stay true to yourself.
there are so many things you'll be celebrating soon.

"*The world breaks everyone, and afterward,
many are strong at the broken places.*"

— ERNEST HEMINGWAY

TO THE THINGS THAT MAKE YOU

pay homage,
to nights that made you question your existence

to daydreams,
that turned into the things you show up for today

to people,
who left you with no inkling of care, only
to be replaced by your soul tribe

to your heart,
which never stopped beating nor loving
everything you crossed paths with

to your ancestors,
and honeydew drops in spring
for nothing grows without the roots

to dead lovers,
and parked car convos at three a.m.
teaching you more than you could put into words

to your former self,
who was everything you needed

pay homage to the things that make you

DEAR SELF,

i want more for you,
you are worthy of everything you desire.
i want you to live with no regrets,
to be free,
to rest well.
don't let life's lows keep you from life's highs.
know your life is worth more
than just to be someone's accessory,
or muted souvenir.
you are your only constant
treat yourself as such
your smile frees
your laugh can change the world
you are the sun
even on days
you feel like
you don't deserve the rays.

DYING ART

i don't think i have nailed the artistry of moving on
the art of seeing a new life
unlike the life i knew
and
once imagined for myself.
the dying art of letting go
of expectations
of life's plans
of the past.
i have a fear of new beginnings
and
broken promises.
i envy starting over
but
the life i once knew is coming to an end.
everything i once knew is gone.
everything i once loved is no longer.
everything i once touched is withering
in my hands as we speak.
new beginnings are inevitable

SOUL TIES

i have been dimension to dimension,
vainly searching for unknown depth,
light,
and whatever else i feel a soul tie to.
soul ties, shit,
the root of all things puzzling.
attachment, the root of all suffering.

LIFE'S CHOICES

i am disappointed but not surprised at the choice you made
you always were a believer in the grass
being greener on the other side
but
i always knew the grass was green where you water it.
i loved you more than i loved myself sometimes.
i was okay with the bare minimum.
i was content with just a crumb,
just the weekends,
just a text.
it left me wanting to be her in an unusual way.
what does she have i don't?
what does she say i won't?
i could've been all you needed.
life's choices have me defeated.
don't you get it?
i would've killed for you
but you chose her
i'm over it
i'm gone.

WORDS I WISH I HEARD

it is okay to mourn what you have lost
it is okay to cry
it is okay to not be okay

you don't have to be strong all the time.
no need to hide your pain
it is okay not to explain

it is okay to not feel pretty every day
and after all,
who does?

VOW TO SELF

i owe it to myself to love me unconditionally.
to find comfort in this.
to know all the answers are within.

i owe it to myself to never go back.
to anything that didn't serve me.
anything that drained me to the point of no return.

i owe it to myself to honor my growth,
for i will never be the same version of myself twice.
i owe it to myself to choose me.

WO(MEN)

silly me,
to think my existence meant anything more
to you than a feminine lightness.
do i stroke your ego?
do i make you feel manly?
do you like how i ride you?
what a lesser man to ever think a woman was lesser than.

this is my third lifetime—
i have seen the fight for suffrage,
watched us crawl our way up from nothing to feel worthy
while getting pushed down
and still,
i am utterly unimpressed.
where is the chivalry?
where are the unearthly men?
the unprogrammed?
the untouched?

as i touch myself,
i realize women play both roles; we are in fact wo(men)
half hell raised,
half feminine.
daughter of Oshun.
when will we understand our power?
society is against us, aren't they?
we terrify them.
isn't it draining to possess all the
power yet feel so powerless?
being the source for the narrow-minded,
the light for the lost souls

–

to lose us is to lose touch

silly me,
for thinking the future is female.

A CONFESSION YOU'LL
NEVER RECEIVE

i don't know how to respond to you these days.
our words don't resonate.
your eyes
don't tell me what i need to know anymore.
i have sat in questioning for a while now,
wrapped in lust time and time again.

you say you love me, but i don't feel it anymore.
you smile at your phone,
but
i'm in front of you.

who are you texting?

you don't call me beautiful,
so i don't feel i am anymore.

you don't get excited to talk to me these days.
i can feel the change with every word uttered.
i can't find the words to ask the inevitable:

have you found someone?

i feel like we're
both just here,
holding space, wasting air,
questioning one another while questioning ourselves.

where did we go wrong?

i think we moved too fast.
found parts of each other too fast.

you touched me
in places
i didn't get to first.

you held space
in places
i didn't know existed.

i found myself resenting you for it.
i wanted to discover me.
so when you told me about myself,
i couldn't argue.
you were there first.
i don't know what parts are really me,
or just a made-up version to fit your reality.

i can't do this anymore.

RETURNING TO LOVE

my love is something i crave but can't seem to give myself.
i envy people who are loved by me.

fearless, selfless, and free

i love my love
yet
deprive myself

am i unworthy of the feeling i freely give to others?

i try my best to be lovable enough these days
i try to feel worthy of my love
try to be more present with myself

more soft
more forgiving
more understanding
more accepting of my love

more, just more.

STRANGER LOVE

sometimes i crave connection to a stranger with no ties
that way you know you really are wanted.
no ties mean no pretending,
right?

i yearn to bare my soul to someone
i might not see tomorrow
sometimes i crave to experience something
i wouldn't care about losing,
a whatever- type of thing.

sometimes a stranger is a perfect dose of what you need,
detached enough to not see your internal flaws
but
close enough to see how beautiful you are
to kiss you with no plans of tomorrow
a present connection
where nothing else matters
but right now,
right now meaning fun,
and fun meaning no heartbreak
at least that's what i crave.
maybe i just like the beginning stages of love.
i hate when "what's your name?" turns into
"i'll be home late tonight"
or
when "no, you hang up first" turns into
"i'm too tired to talk tonight."

i hate becoming the norm for anyone.
i crave stranger love.

STILL

i am tired of writing love letters with no end.
tired of you talking to me like i'm disposable.
i owe myself an apology for not owning myself sooner.
i put myself on the back burner for a while.
it's been a minute since i have sat with myself,
been a minute since i've been able to feel my feelings.

a minute,
all i need is one,
to prove to myself
i'm still mortal
still breathing
still here
still worthy of a love that
doesn't require pain to validate
one i don't have to heal from
one that reminds me of my potential

i want that.
i deserve that.

it's been a minute since i said this out loud,
a lifetime since i actually believed it.
i have nothing to lose.
everything to gain.
i lack nothing.

BROWN-SKINNED GIRL

brown-skinned girl,
you are so special.
from your coils to your curves
down to your toes
your skin is melanin armor
with shields of strength
and
wings of gold.

i would do anything for you.

you must learn to love you to your core,
because this world wasn't made
for you to love and explore.
brown girl, take a rest.
i know the world expects you
to carry their troubles on your neck

breathe, reset, i see you.

i think we all get to a pivotal point of shedding.
shedding old habits, relationships, ideals, and
previous versions of ourselves. for some, it may
have been a specific situation, feeling, or person
who triggered this change. however, i believe it is
important to pinpoint where that shift takes place
and what exactly inspires our paths and growth.

life is in constant motion and stops
for no one, not even you.

growth and comfort do not mix. growth requires
us to challenge the boundaries of what is known.
it takes to get out of our comfort zone, to make
mistakes by definition, to be uncomfortable,
and not run away from the discomfort.

"get comfortable with being uncomfortable."

you may occupy days where you see and feel only
yourself, your mishaps, and your future. i consider
these *"self-reflect"* days. when these days come,
you look around only to discover you looking back
at yourself. this is merely the key moment for
necessary change; this by heart represents the
moment to cultivate another expanded version
of you and to shed what no longer serves you.

be intentional about who you want to be and what
spaces you want to occupy when it's all said and done.

you can reinvent yourself as many
times as you want in this life.
you choose who you want to be,
every day.

— lessons i've learnt about becoming

MIRROR REFLECTIONS

leave people softer than you met them
water their spirit and add layers to their being.

you attract your mirrors in every season.
as you teach, you learn.
as you accept, you ascend.

every soul you encounter is going to show you yourself

what's there.
what's missing.
what's dead.
what's present.

embrace the reflections and leave them softer.

MAY TOMORROW

may tomorrow bring you what you need,
rising like a phoenix with the morning sun,
leaving yesterday's troubles in the ashes.
may hell get nervous when you start your day.
may you meet yourself in a past life and realize
you are everything you say you are
and more.
you deserve abundance.
you are abundant.
the best of you is ahead of you.
may tomorrow remind you of these truths.

TIMELESS ACTS

i am learning every word that comes
out of our mouths is vital
for asking the right question
or
for declaring a precise thing is an art form.
only give life to words that are going to be
timeless,
memorable,
and
worthy of being contributed to the air.
affirm yourself and others,
speak life unto dead dreams.
i am aware our tongue is a sword and can cut deep
but can also heal.
i am still learning to utilize it for the right things.

DAY TWO BLUES

it's day two,
and the feelings of anger have disappeared with the sun.
now i'm just hurt,
in disbelief you didn't choose me.

in this moment
i'm stuck with the feeling of "not good enough"
but it's just for now
sooner or later i'll be too good.
what feelings will arise on day three?
i can't be too sure
but
today is our anniversary,
and
i can't bring myself to care.
just like you couldn't bring yourself to respect me.

i wanted my flowers while alive.
i wanted more out of love.

time heals all,
new days bring new feelings,
and
today on day two,
i'm hurt.

WELCOME YOUR HEALING

healing is **not** linear
nor is it something i can explain without laying
down my burdens and facing myself.
healing is done in layers.
you peel one back and find a dozen more,
waiting to be reassured and restored,
things you thought you cleared will rise
again like the morning sun.
every day is an opportunity to show up differently

welcome your healing

the answers you need will find their way home.

ECLIPSED EXISTENCE

who are you going to be when it's all over?
when the sun sets and,
you're alone with your thoughts.
no movement to redeem you,
just stillness.
like a body of water in meditation.

when the moon mounts a display of all your insecurities.
when the sun isn't there to liberate you.
just you, in all your darkness.
when you can't hide behind anything,
your humor,
your fears,
your wit.
when all is said and done
who are you going to be?

HONEST PROGRESS

my heart is heavy,
yet my third eye is wired open.
i don't know if i am ready
to experience anyone other than myself
in this season of my life
and
i think that is okay.

it is okay to only want to cater to yourself.
it is okay if no one else claps for you.
it is okay to be alone.
there is identity in the solitude,
a message of reassurance in the silence.
you find peace in the gray areas,
and the souls who speak your language,
find you in the words left unsaid.

in the blank spaces,
you find yourself

ready to fill in the spaces you left for others.

it is okay
to save yourself.

HALF & HALF

love, to me,
symbolizes everything
and
nothing at the same time.
having everything when love is on your side
but having nothing
when this love decides to leave or becomes lost.
i've been questioning the balance of love for a while now.

how can you love someone and still hurt them?

love is a lie and the truth
yin and the yang
hell and heaven
being lost for words and can't stop talking
first hello to the last goodbye.

love is balance.

love is a blessing and a curse.
is it god or the devil's work?

did they mix and make such a
bittersweet four-lettered word?

you can't do without it
but
with it you are blinded
can't think straight.
you are never sober when you're in love.
it's the best trip,
but when it comes to an end,
you are searching for your reason to love again.
like russian roulette,
never knowing
which bullet will be the one to shatter
your pretty little heart
and
have you questioning what love is.

SOUL QUEST

most of the time, i look inside
and find the answers waiting; they come with ease.
in your season of stillness, stand in your power,
validate yourself,
you are what you seek,
don't be afraid of the solitude,
that comes with what you need.

ONE-SIDED LOVE

i'm always the one that holds on:
the one who must have the last word,
the one on the other end of the call
saying "you hang up first."

i'm always the one left wondering,
seeking an answer,
bleeding out.

love is my only weakness,
but it's always one-sided,
and i'm the one left loving.

I FORGOT TO TELL YOU

i am done apologizing
for finding myself in the midst of your absence,
for not needing you.
i am done apologizing for not being
good enough in your eyes,
when you didn't even know what good was,
let alone when enough was enough.
no apologies for not sticking around,
when your words became slurred,

and the promises got blurred,
by too many names i couldn't pronounce.

i deal with enough just being a woman.
i am not sorry for no longer putting
up with the shit i used to take.
i am finally done apologizing for choosing me.

THE PRAYER

i tried to find my answered prayer in your betrayal.
my muse in your deception.
my voice in you leaving.

i wanted,
to be what you needed.
i prayed,
to be someone you prayed for.
i tried,
to write a love song that ended in your eulogy.

i tried for you.

MIRROR CONFESSIONS

i don't know if i ever told you this
but
i loved you.

i admired everything about you,
your sense of self
your demeanor
the way hell got nervous when you uttered a word.
i loved the way you showed up in the world
and even more,
how you made space for me to show up authentically.

i even loved me while with you.
you touched me in places no ex-lover could.
for that, my soul was wide open to you.

you saw me.
for the brief time you stayed,
i didn't have to explain my soul
or
words my heart felt but couldn't speak aloud.
you knew.
your presence alone made my inner child feel safe,
catered to, like i had a place.
it left me softer,
confirming what i always knew:
i was not hard to love.

WORTH THE WAIT

the wait will be worth it.
it will come wrapped in everything you prayed for,
looking exactly how you imagined it.
no pain attached,
no used strings.
you are worthy of the love you seek.
you don't have to explain why you deserve it.

A NOTE FOR YOUR RISING

that night,
i left you a note for your rising.
inside i wrote:
21 times you abandoned me for a man,
one for every year i circled the earth.
even though our flesh was interconnected since birth,
i knew i wasn't your chosen one
i knew you would choose him every day after this
and
i was right.
i dreaded this night.
i felt the betrayal
i felt the hurt
i felt the choice you made
and
it wasn't me.
i never understood
but
i have a life to live.

i hope this note found you exactly where i left you:
under a man you would always choose.

CLARITY COMES IN THE MORNING

today is the day
i let my thoughts
come and stay
i don't force them away
i didn't run from them either
other days they were fleeting
though times before they were non-existent
but
today must be the day they came to stay

my memory of us has been distorted for a while now
today is the day i let the memories of us take root in my mind
and
i think i am finally ready to unpack them.

i started demanding why
knowing the countless outcomes that could come from this
three-letter word
why did it end?
why did you lie?
why am i the one left cursing at the sky?

most of the time these thoughts come with the wavering and
melancholy feelings of baseless complaint followed by feeling less than
but these thoughts were different
these thoughts came with needed answers and solutions
they came with clarity.

clarity comes when i intentionally set boundaries.

clarity comes when i learn how to say no.

clarity comes when i stop dating potential.

clarity comes with every new day the sun rises.

clarity comes when i let my thoughts stay.

SEASONAL SOULS

it gets better.
i'm saying this because i live it.
i live mornings where the essence of
my purpose gets me out of bed.
everything aligns,
everything makes sense,
and the sun shines again
you're who you remember yourself to be
before life got to you,
before others' views tainted how you viewed yourself.
you will laugh so hard you cry,
you will meet people who mirror all your good,
your blessings will overflow because you stayed,
stayed on this earth
and stayed true to yourself.
people will leave, yes.
but that is a blessing.
see it as such.
the people meant for you will find you in every season.
don't let seasonal souls overstay their welcome
the blessings are in the loss.

PEOPLE AREN'T HOMES

i wish i knew then what i know now:
your recycled words were nothing
but a faint hope of eternity.
an eternity
i longed for and didn't know existed
until i encountered you.
after our intricate dance around the moon,
no one could tell me you weren't heaven-sent.

i wish i knew this vain hope was a hoax,
a beautiful hoax,
one that made me fall so deep,
i was convinced everyone should
experience this one dance,
no matter how short,
no matter how raw,
no matter how it hurt.

until our dance came to an end,
for a second i almost wanted to keep pretending—
pretending you were the one.
i thought there was life in your eyes,
but really they were reflecting mine.
i wanted this dance to be mutual
but
really i was hauling you.
my arms became weary,
and
you were just along for the ride.

I NAMED US GRIEF

no one could save me from myself,
not even you.
yet,
you always tried.

anxiously tried to calm my demons
forcibly tried to negotiate with my depression
frantically tried to reason with my trauma.

yet,
it ended exactly how i expected.
you were forced to heal because of me.
you tried even when i was weakening you.
the never-ending circle
the never-ending push and pull

i desperately wish i could have spared you.
but i was drowning myself.
i told you
you couldn't save me.

SURVIVOR'S GUILT

i am sorry
i couldn't make this life more livable for you.
sorry you had to heal from this hurt.
i'm sorry you had to pray to gods you
stopped believing in lifetimes ago.

i know this all too well.

i know bloody wrists and locked doors.
i know broken bottles and screams so
horrid they turn to silenced screams.

journals get filled up
because life got too surreal.
carrying a suicide note like a pen
because you were a ticking time bomb.

i know this all too well.

i know
what it feels like
to be almost certain
death would be better than this.

but

AIN'T I A SURVIVOR ?

SELF MONOLOGUE

i have moved on,
with intent this time.
i am no longer easily impressed,
no longer lingering,
no longer settling,
for you.
i am whole by myself.
i have discovered me for myself.
i am me all by myself.
i am no longer looking outside of myself

i keep my heart on my sleeve,
with no shame now.
my heart is ready to give,
with no fear of drowning.
i can save myself now,
i move with intent now.
i utter my mumbling thoughts with conviction,
because i am convicted now
with the essence of moving on.

I'VE LEARNED

i look at you and see me.
i see all the times you beat me down with unkind words,
twisting things i said in a fight,
telling the world how i cried in your lap last summer,
and how i was weak for it.
the shame carried over,
and the pain got lost in between words you
thought were necessary to humble me.
i cried for days after; my soul ached for a lifetime.
i've learned to move on without an apology.
i revisit these words occasionally.
they hurt the same
but
still, i stayed,
thinking one day i could make you love me,
make you see i was the one,
make you take these words back so i could finally move on.
i'm done letting tears fall for someone
who doesn't love themselves.
if you did,
you could see you didn't deserve me.

DAMAGED EXPECTATIONS

i lost myself when i lost sight of reality.
i lost myself in wanting you,
lost even more in you not wanting me.

i lost the definition i was always fed of love.
i grew up thinking
love could never hurt you,
love would never leave.

i expected a never-ending summer romance with you.
i expected picnics in the wind.
i expected my cheeks to hurt from smiling.

love is not what i expected it to be.

i was bathed in the essence of detachment,
re-birthed in a sense of knowing

in knowing,
you weren't worth my loss.
you weren't worth my death.
you weren't worth my love.

it is time to welcome myself back home.

EPITOME

i am the epitome of bittersweet,
for this life has been nothing but
a reminder i am a mistake,

an oh-so-sweet mistake.

i want my heart taken out of my body,
for this is a useless piece that has done me no good.
my body burned to ashes,
and spread across every place where i felt less than,
which was every place i stepped foot in,
including this one,
where i stand on a stool,
waiting for something to click
and
remind me it is too late to be what i could've been.

WHAT A TIME

it is pivotal for us to honor our season,
hold space for our feelings.
rebirths are inevitable.
what a time to be a phoenix.

TAKE IT OR LEAVE IT

i have been confronting my demons alone for years.
some days are worse than others,
and today was a dreadful day.
i couldn't bring myself to love you, let alone myself.
i wait for you to tell me if you can deal with this or not,
dealing with my demons always adding their two cents,
loving me while loving them too.
i understand either way.
this battle is not for the weak,
and you seem to be someone too perfect to want to suit up.
you either take me as raw as i am
or
entrust me with my demons.
at least they let me be me.

TURTLENECK SUMMERS

the first time,
you swore it was the last.

i never knew you to break your word so i held you to it
i knew it broke you that love hurt you
especially from a partner
and i didn't want you to relive it,

so i kept quiet.

the second time,
you called me crying at 3 am,
said
you needed someone to talk to
said you needed a friend
of course,
i came through
with the wine
and
the booze;
you know how we do.

we talked until the sun came up.
you said you didn't know why—

why you stayed
why he lied

you left me with a promise
no more pain
no more bruises
no more turtlenecks in the summer
no more music to cover up the screams

the third time,
you left me a voicemail saying this was it
how you packed your bags for real this time
but he wasn't having it

you said you never saw him like this.

pacing
back
and
forth
i could hear it in your voice
that you knew you weren't gonna
make it out this time alive

i swear i heard a gunshot but i wasn't sure.
i raced to your house, passing every light insight.
the police beat me to it
said the neighbors called for excessive screams
i told them i was your sister
and
demanded to see the scene
i was confident i would walk in
and
hear you talking about a next time.

but instead,
i saw you in a pool of blood waiting to be identified.
i saw him lying next to you with a gun in his hand,
both lifeless—

i was speechless
i held you in my arms and cried.
the first time,
you swore it was the last

FLOW WITHOUT FORCE

you have come a long way.
you finally recognize the person in the mirror.

i applaud you
for no longer settling for spaces or relationships
that don't allow you to be seen, heard, or felt.

zero force, just alignment.

finally,
seeking out voices that speak to who you are becoming.
stepping into your power.
the best thing you can do for yourself is stay true to you.

there are so many things you'll be celebrating soon.

SIGNED, THE PHOENIX

you will thank yourself in a love letter
for how far you have come.
you will stamp it
with all the trials you overcame,
the rebirths
you inevitably encountered,
and
all the hopeless tears that have fallen
you will thank the people who left you
shattered
to discover yourself in the scattered pieces.
you will seal this love letter with roses,
one for every piece of you found in the ashes.
you will thank yourself for living out your potential
and
decoding the hidden messages in the betrayal.
the fear of the unknown will be confirmed in this letter
everything happened the way it was intended.

thank you for embracing you.

it was worth it.
you are worth it.

signed,
the phoenix.

"*Not everyone survives; thank you for surviving.*"

—TYLER JOSEPH

ACKNOWLEDGMENTS

when setting out on a long journey you've never embarked on before, you never know how much work it will take to reach your final destination. i've discovered along my journey writing *manipulated memories* publishing a book takes a village, and i am so grateful for all the support. fulfilling this dream would not have been possible without you.

thank you to those who donated and pre-ordered:

the anthony family, the ramlochans, the joseph family, the colemans, candice thomas, chelsea nnorom, joshua wilks, kemba hendrix, samara dixon, monica floyd, sean williams, iyawnna wilson, crystal e hunter, stephen watts, anthony black-bush, anjali chinsammy, santana vaughan, ikenna nebo, quinn doyle, jonquille rice, shanella gandharry, eric koester, aik imoekor, zhanae featherston, deejh, nikki lawrence, jeremiah williams (rudy), brittany hubbard, shae dobson, rachel mcbride, bethany baptiste, kd saunders, xcarl macki, deesha philyaw, ian nesbitt, daud mumin, jade blaise, kwentoria williams, luka haidome, tony shivdyal, alan soto, davore thomas, michael hurtado, kimberly straub, lori kaplan, emily o'neil, alaina briceland-betts, andrea m elganzoury, kelly e long, beverly wehmer-kumari, nadine vatel, bam byrd, pamela bakel, william pree, rachel motley, destin bryant, desiree barnes, vannita piedu, portia white, jayla ford, divine faith, chiquita jackson, labarbara amaker, devyn cooks, ayanni seay, sherah salter, nafeesah risdon, janay james, crystal e hunter, jordan mcdonald, blanca coello, belle glass, diana kerolos, stone brickhouse, alphonso bonds jr, denise contreras, tracey higgs, zania colar, carol smith, arnaijah bryant, arielle mitchell, gene celesse, ugo amoretti, tamira dickens, kai scott